PANDORA'S BOX

By Nick Saunders
Consultant: Dr. Thorsten Opper, Curator of Greek and Roman Antiquities, British Museum, London

Please visit our web site at www.garethstevens.com
For a free color catalog describing our list of high-quality books, call 1-800-542-2595 (USA) or 1-800-387-3178 (Canada).
Our fax 1-877-542-2596.

Library of Congress Cataloging-in-Publication Data available upon request from publisher.
Fax (414) 336-0157 for the attention of the Publishing Records Department.

ISBN-10: 0-8368-7747-0 ISBN-13: 978-0-8368-7747-2 (lib. bdg.)
ISBN-10: 0-8368-8147-8 ISBN-13: 978-0-8368-8147-9 (softcover)

This North America edition first published in 2007 by
World Almanac® Library
An Imprint of Gareth Stevens Publishing
1 Reader's Digest Road
Pleasantville, NY 10570-7000 USA

Illustrators: Bookmatrix

World Almanac® Library managing editor: Valerie J. Weber
World Almanac® Library editor: Leifa Butrick
World Almanac® Library art direction: Tammy West

Manufactured in the United States of America

CPSIA Compliance Information: Batch #CR012101GS: For further information contact Gareth Stevens, New York, New York at 1-800-542-2595

CONTENTS

THE GREEKS, THEIR GODS, & MYTHS

The world of the ancient Greeks was bound by the Mediterranean Sea and the rugged lands surrounding it. It was a place of dangerous winds and sudden storms. The ancient Greeks saw their lives as controlled by spirits of nature and the gods. They told myths about how the gods fought with each other and created the universe. These stories helped explain what caused natural events, such as lightning and earthquakes, and the fates of individuals.

The ancient Greeks believed that 12 gods and goddesses ruled over the world. The gods and goddesses shown on the next page are the most important ones. Some of them appear in this myth.

The ancient Greek gods and goddesses looked and acted like human beings. They fell in love, were jealous and vain, and argued with each other. But unlike humans, they were immortal. They did not die but lived forever. They also had superhuman strength and specific magical powers. Each god or goddess controlled certain forces of nature or aspects of human life, such as marriage or hunting.

In the myths, the gods had their favorite humans. Sometimes, the gods even had children with these people. Their children were thus half gods.

They were usually mortal, which meant that they could die. It also meant that they had some special powers, too. When their human children were in trouble, the gods would help them.

The gods li[illegible] to meddle in human life and took side[illegible]erent people. The gods also liked to pl[illegible] humans. They did so for many rea[illegible]use it was fun; because they wo[illegible]thing; or because they wanted [illegible] with someone.

Olympus.

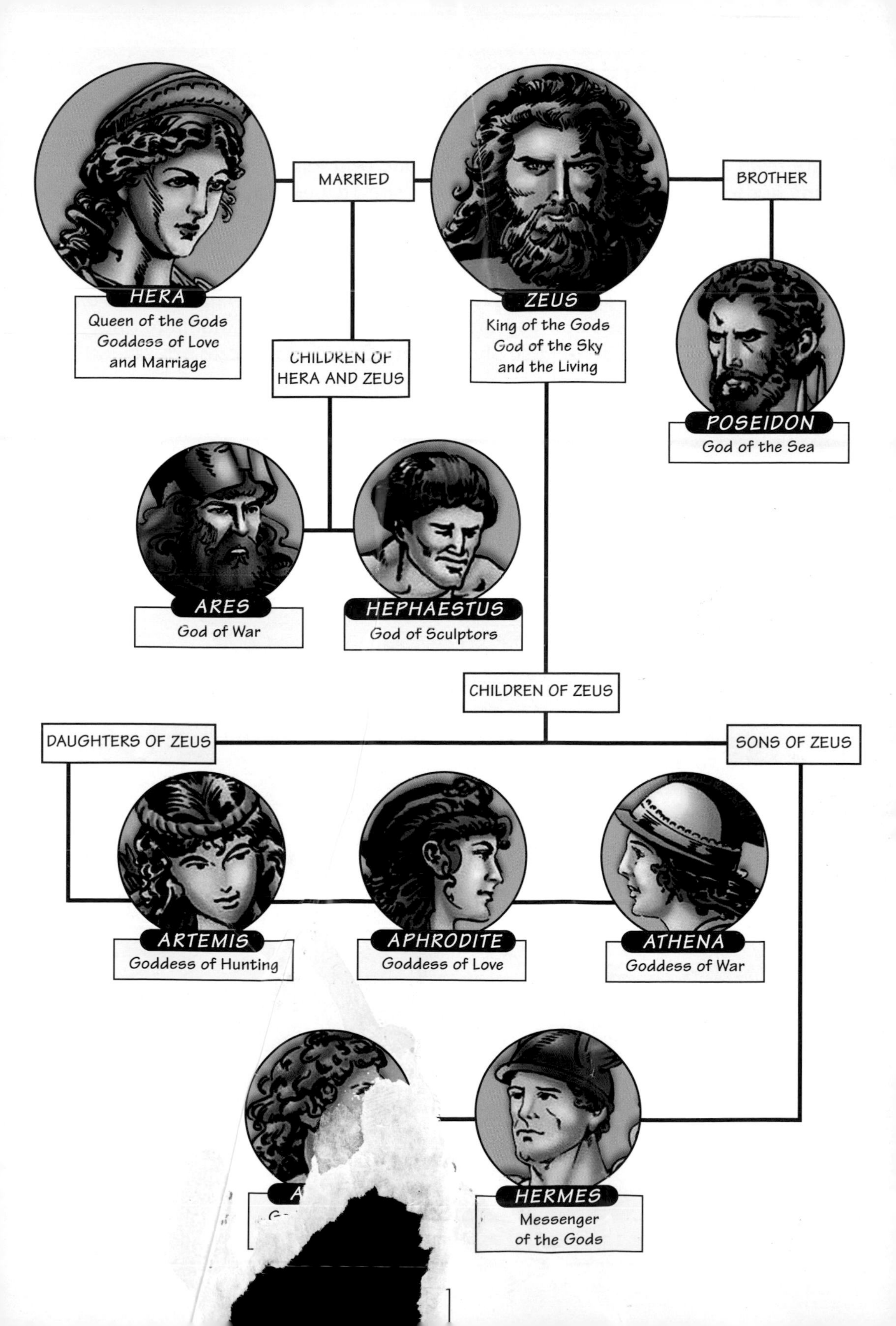
HERA
Queen of the Gods
Goddess of Love
and Marriage
MARRIED
ZEUS
King of the Gods
God of the Sky
and the Living
BROTHER
POSEIDON
God of the Sea
CHILDREN OF
HERA AND ZEUS
ARES
God of War
HEPHAESTUS
God of Sculptors
CHILDREN OF ZEUS
DAUGHTERS OF ZEUS
SONS OF ZEUS
ARTEMIS
Goddess of Hunting
APHRODITE
Goddess of Love
ATHENA
Goddess of War
HERMES
Messenger
of the Gods

HOW THE MYTH BEGINS

Where did men and women come from, and who created them? Before the gods from Mount Olympus ruled the heavens and earth, another race of giant gods was in charge. They were called the Titans. Two of the Titans, Prometheus and his brother Epimetheus, created men and the animals of Earth. Prometheus stole fire from Zeus and the other gods from Mount Olympus and gave it to men. Zeus was very angry at the theft and said he would get revenge. He created Pandora, the first woman. He gave her a box full of evil spirits. These spirits would bring suffering to all humans and make them mortal. According to the ancient Greeks, the gods affect human life itself. No one can escape both sadness and happiness.

According to the myths, the gods lived on Mount

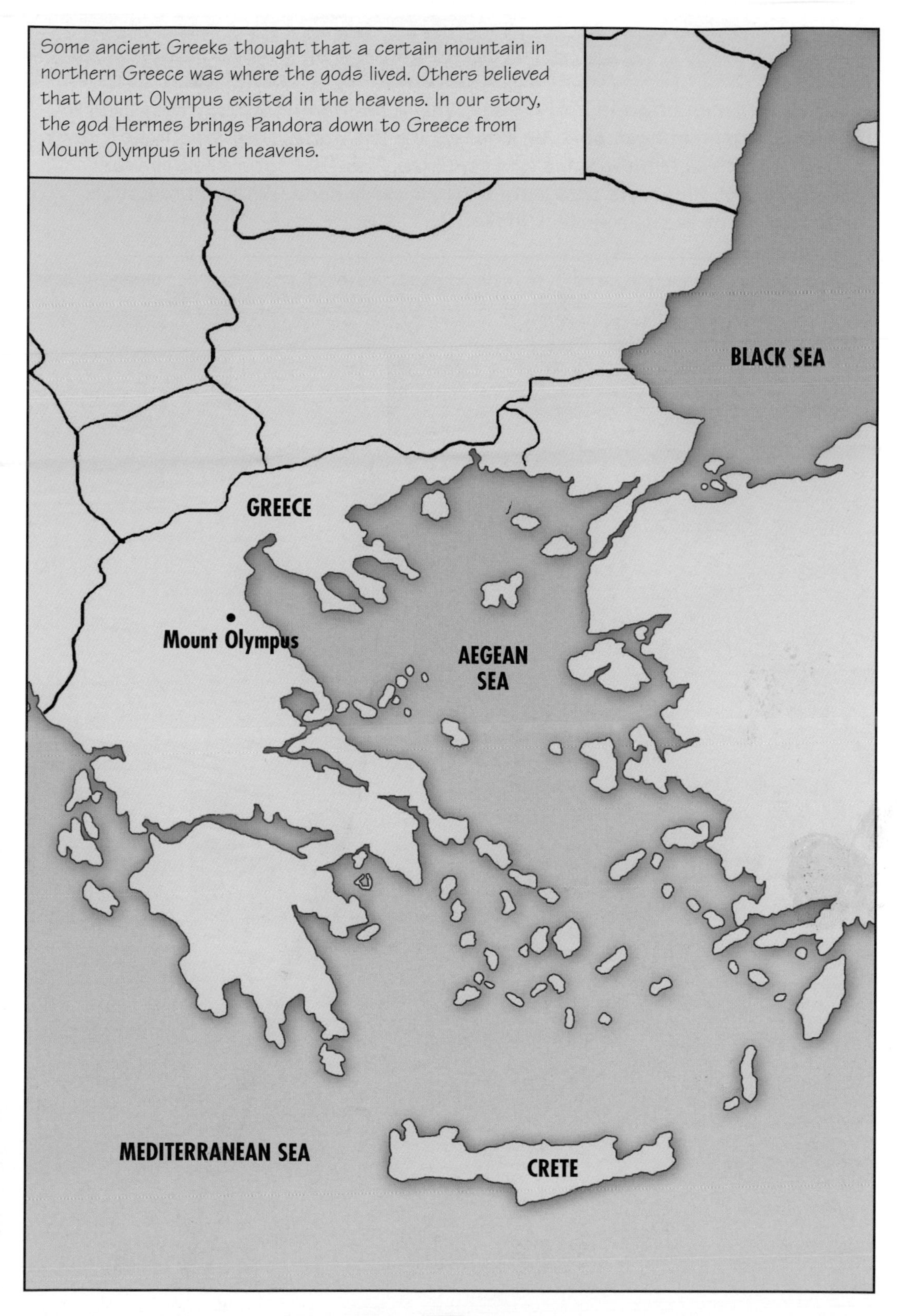
Some ancient Greeks thought that a certain mountain in northern Greece was where the gods lived. Others believed that Mount Olympus existed in the heavens. In our story, the god Hermes brings Pandora down to Greece from Mount Olympus in the heavens.
BLACK SEA
GREECE
Mount Olympus
AEGEAN SEA
MEDITERRANEAN SEA
CRETE

A PERFECT LIFE

In the early times of gods and heroes, only men lived on Earth. They lived a life without pain, hunger, cold, or illness. Like the gods, they also lived forever. It was a time free from worries and troubles. The Titan god Prometheus looked after the men. He took care of their every need. What more could these men want in their perfect life?

The men lived peacefully in their world. Food was plentiful, and life was easy. The only thing they lacked was fire for cooking food and for light and warmth in the evening.

Look, Hera, see how happy these men are.
Yes, my lord. What is Prometheus doing, running so fast?
Hoping to make life for men even better, Prometheus stole the gods' fire. Men could now cook food, enjoy warmth when it was cold, and have light when the Sun went down.
I will give this fire to men. They will have all they want then.

Zeus, king of the gods, was angry with Prometheus for stealing the gods' prized fire. So he chained Prometheus to a mountain. Every day, a huge, ugly vulture pecked at Prometheus's body. Every night, Prometheus's wounds healed, but every day, the vulture returned to bite him again.
Prometheus, the gods' fire was never meant for mere humans.
Aarrgh! How long will I be punished like this?

One day, Zeus's son, the super-strong Hercules, heard Prometheus's scream. Always ready to help people in pain, Hercules rushed to help him. He killed the vulture and broke Prometheus's chains.

The news of Prometheus's escape angered Zeus. He wandered around his palace on Mount Olympus, thinking up another punishment for Prometheus.

THE FIRST WOMAN

Zeus thought of a clever and cruel punishment for Prometheus and mankind. He would offer them a gift that appeared perfect on the outside. Once they took the gift, it would ruin their happy world. He needed the help of all the gods for his plan to work. First, he called on Hephaestus, god of sculptors. Zeus told him to make a person from clay.

Zeus was very happy when Hephaestus showed him his sculpture. His creation was stunning. Now, Zeus called his daughter, Athena, to bring the statue to life.
Athena, breathe life into this woman so she can live on Earth.
Yes, Father. But how can such a beautiful woman be a punishment to men?

Now Zeus needed the other gods and goddesses to play their parts in his clever plan. He called them to his palace. He asked each one to give his wonderful creation a gift.

Come, my children, each of you must give this woman a magical gift.
I give you great beauty and womanly grace to charm all men.
My plan is working well. That is a fine gift from Aphrodite, goddess of love!

Hermes was the messenger of the gods and knew what men were like. He thought that this beautiful woman would have to be smart.
My gift will help you understand the thoughts of men.
Hermes, this is a wonderful gift. I know nothing of the ways of men.
Athena knew that this woman needed practical skills such as sewing, spinning, and weaving to help her survive.
I have already given you the breath of life, but I will now teach you to sew.
Slowly, the woman was becoming the perfect gift for mankind.

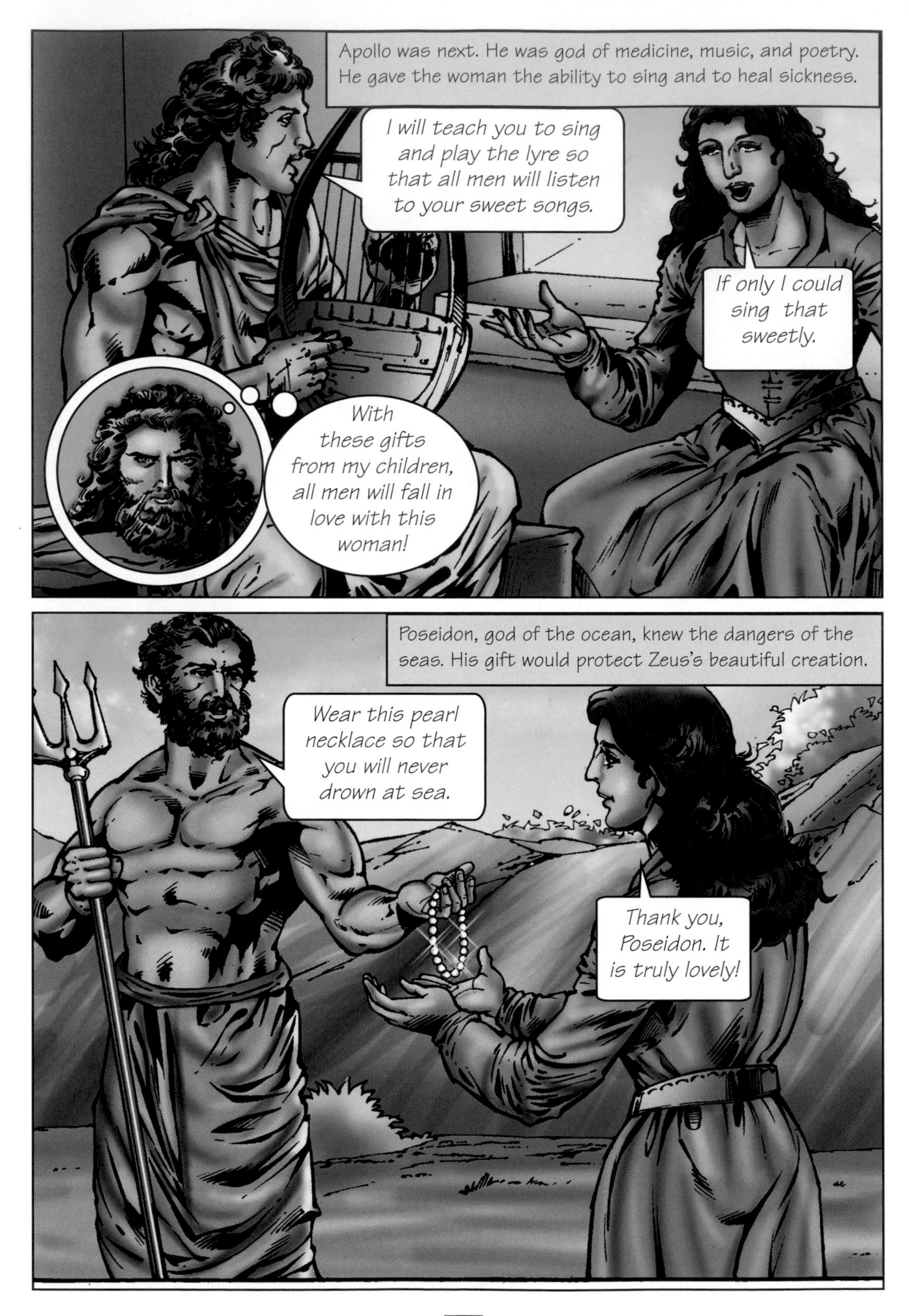
Apollo was next. He was god of medicine, music, and poetry. He gave the woman the ability to sing and to heal sickness.
I will teach you to sing and play the lyre so that all men will listen to your sweet songs.
If only I could sing that sweetly.
With these gifts from my children, all men will fall in love with this woman!
Poseidon, god of the ocean, knew the dangers of the seas. His gift would protect Zeus's beautiful creation.
Wear this pearl necklace so that you will never drown at sea.
Thank you, Poseidon. It is truly lovely!

Finally, it was Zeus's turn to give Pandora a gift.
What gift do you have for me, Zeus?
I told them to create you. Now I will name you Pandora, which means "gifted with all."
I will also make you lazy and full of mischief.

Zeus ordered a great feast to be held on Mount Olympus. The gods and goddesses came to see Pandora, and each one gave her a secret. Hephaestus, the sculptor, had created a magical box to hold these secrets. A glittering golden cord kept the box safely shut.

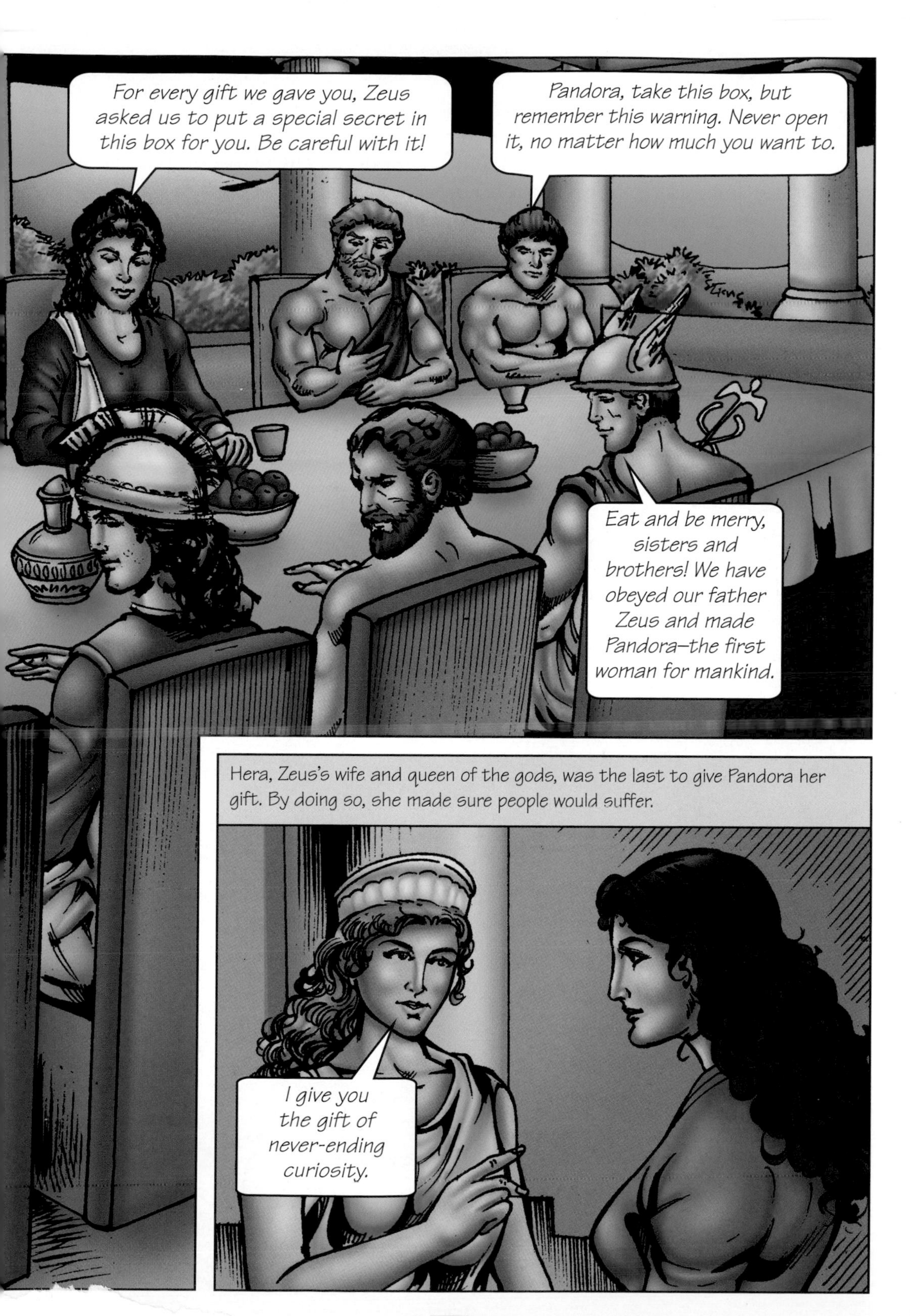
For every gift we gave you, Zeus asked us to put a special secret in this box for you. Be careful with it!
Pandora, take this box, but remember this warning. Never open it, no matter how much you want to.
Eat and be merry, sisters and brothers! We have obeyed our father Zeus and made Pandora—the first woman for mankind.
Hera, Zeus's wife and queen of the gods, was the last to give Pandora her gift. By doing so, she made sure people would suffer.
I give you the gift of never-ending curiosity.

A NEW LIFE

It was now time for Pandora to begin her new life on Earth. Hermes helped Pandora down the steep sides of Mount Olympus to the world of men. He showed her the way to Prometheus's home. How would she cope in this strange place away from the gods? Would their gifts help her? And what of the secrets inside her magical box?

Pandora and Hermes did not receive a warm welcome. Prometheus was worried about Zeus's gift and wouldn't marry Pandora. He told his brother, Epimetheus, to ignore Pandora, too.

Prometheus, Zeus wishes you to have this woman, Pandora. He made her specially for you.
Hermes, I thank you and your lord Zeus. But this present is too great. I cannot accept it.

But Epimetheus was not as wise as his brother. The charms Aphrodite had given Pandora worked on him. Epimetheus was fooled by her beauty.

Oh great Epimetheus, my lord Zeus offers you this special gift—a woman called Pandora.
Thank Zeus for me. I accept this wonderful gift and will make her my wife.

Epimetheus fell deeply in love with Pandora. He was blinded by her charm and beauty, and soon they were married.
See how Pandora's gifts are starting to work?
Oh Pandora! The gods have made you perfect in every way. I am very happy.
Well done, Hermes! You have succeeded in your task.
At first, Pandora and Epimetheus lived a wonderful life. They had each other. It was all they needed in their lives.
Epimetheus, my dearest husband, my life is complete.

The happy couple walked hand in hand. They picked flowers, danced, played the lyre, and ate sweet fruits. What could possibly make them unhappy?
Pandora, take these flowers for your hair. Their smell is as sweet as the sound of your voice.
My life is as good as the gods' lives.

Each day, Pandora polished her sparkling magical box. Although Hera had given her curiosity, Pandora had not opened the box. But she really wanted to know what was inside.

Can Pandora overcome her desire to open her box?

She cannot hold out for ever.

I haven't seen such a beautiful box anywhere. Surely it must keep some beautiful things safe. But I must remember Hephaestus's warning.

Each day, Pandora's curiosity grew and grew. She started to think that she could hear voices in the box calling out to her.
I'm sure the box is calling me—begging me to open it.
Come, my beautiful Pandora. Let's walk together in the forest.
Pandora! Pandora!
Open the box.
Let us out.
Curiosity started to torture poor Pandora. She imagined that the box contained golden treasures and glittering jewels. If only she could look inside—just once!
What harm could come from taking one look?

As the days went by, Pandora imagined the voices in the box were getting louder. They shouted at her to open the box and set them free.
You cannot ignore them much longer, Pandora!
Aarrgh! I can't stand it. The voices keep begging me to open the box. But I must be strong.
Pandora, set us free!

Pandora knew that she was getting weaker. Once again, she remembered Hephaestus's stern warning. So she hid the box in an old cupboard. Surely, the voices would leave her alone now.

I shall hide the box in here. It will be out of sight, and I won't hear those voices begging me.
Hear me, Pandora. Never open the box. Ignore your curiosity!

But the voices grew louder and louder. They called Pandora's name, trying to get her to open the box.
I will only hold it for a minute.
Pandora, why won't you look at us?
Open the box, Pandora!
Pandora! Let us out to play.

Pandora knew she must fight the urge. But she felt unable to ignore the voices any longer. She put the box in a wooden chest, wrapping it with large iron chains, and closing the lock.
That should do it! It's too hard to open now. I'll wear the key on my necklace, so it is safe.
Pandora was afraid that her will was not strong enough. She did everything she could to hide her box. Would her efforts work? Or would she weaken?
I will bury the chest here in the garden and cover it with a heavy rock.

LIFTING THE LID

Pandora and Epimetheus continued to live a happy life together, but secretly Pandora was troubled by the box. Although the voices no longer spoke constantly, they would still call. One night, the magic box filled her dreams. The voices cried out to her louder than ever. She woke up and crept to the garden, making sure no one saw her.

The big rock that had been hard to move over the chest now magically jumped away. The chest lay in the hole where she had left it. Now the voices were louder than ever before!

Pandora! Free us!
Pandora, set us free!
Pandora, at last you've heard us.

Pandora dug into the soil to lift out the wooden chest. She unlocked the chains and then removed her magical box. She loosened the glittering rope that had held the lid tightly shut.

Uurrgh! What is that nasty smell?

As soon as Pandora opened the box, a high-pitched whiny sound filled the air. She knew right away that she had let something terrible get out.
I knew your gift of curiosity would work, Hera.
Yes, lord Zeus, my gift has delivered your punishment.
I am Misery.
I am Grief.
I am Death.
I am Hunger.

Zeus had insisted that each god place a secret in Pandora's magical box. He said it must be a cruel secret. Pandora now realized this and slammed the box shut. But it was too late.
Greed is my name.
Oh! By the power of Apollo, what have I done?
And I am Disease.
Horrible little winged creatures flew out of the box. They buzzed around Pandora in a terrifying swarm. At last, they were free on Earth.

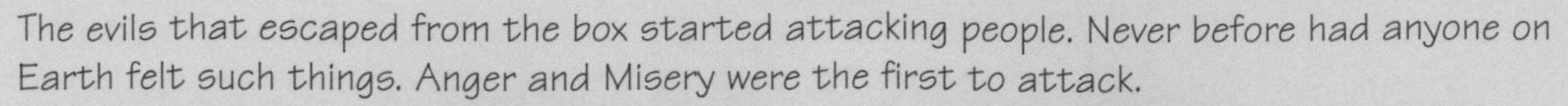
The evils that escaped from the box started attacking people. Never before had anyone on Earth felt such things. Anger and Misery were the first to attack.

What is happening? This is not right.
Epimetheus, I am so sorry. I opened the box and let all these terrible things out!

Epimetheus felt anger for the first time. He shouted at his wife in a wild rage that frightened Pandora. What was wrong with her loving husband?

You silly woman, Pandora! Hephaestus warned you never to open the box! Look at how unhappy you have made us.

Oh, what shall I do? I have never felt so sad.

Sob

Epimetheus's angry shouts made Pandora cry. For the first time in her life, she began to weep with sorrow, not joy.

Soon, the evils that Pandora released from the box flew to every corner of Earth. Everywhere they went, people suffered. People felt pain and grief that they had never known before.
Men are finally punished by our evil secrets.
I hope Prometheus has learned his lesson for stealing our fire.
Why do I feel so bad?
By Zeus, I have never known such feelings.
Anger, illness, disease, passion, greed, lies, jealousy, pain, crime, hunger, old age, death, sorrow, and all the other curses found their way into every house and village. They brought misery to everyone.

Disease and old age struck every home. Everyone felt pain and suffering. There was no escape from the evils that Pandora had released.

Death and grief had also arrived. Along with them came misery and hardship. Instead of living forever, everyone would now die. Soon, funeral pyres burned all over Earth.

IS THERE HOPE?

Epimetheus's anger grew as he realized the terrible pain that Pandora had caused. For the first time, they fought. Now that evil and sorrow were everywhere, human life was hopeless. Even worse, Pandora could still hear a voice from her box. What other misery was hiding there?

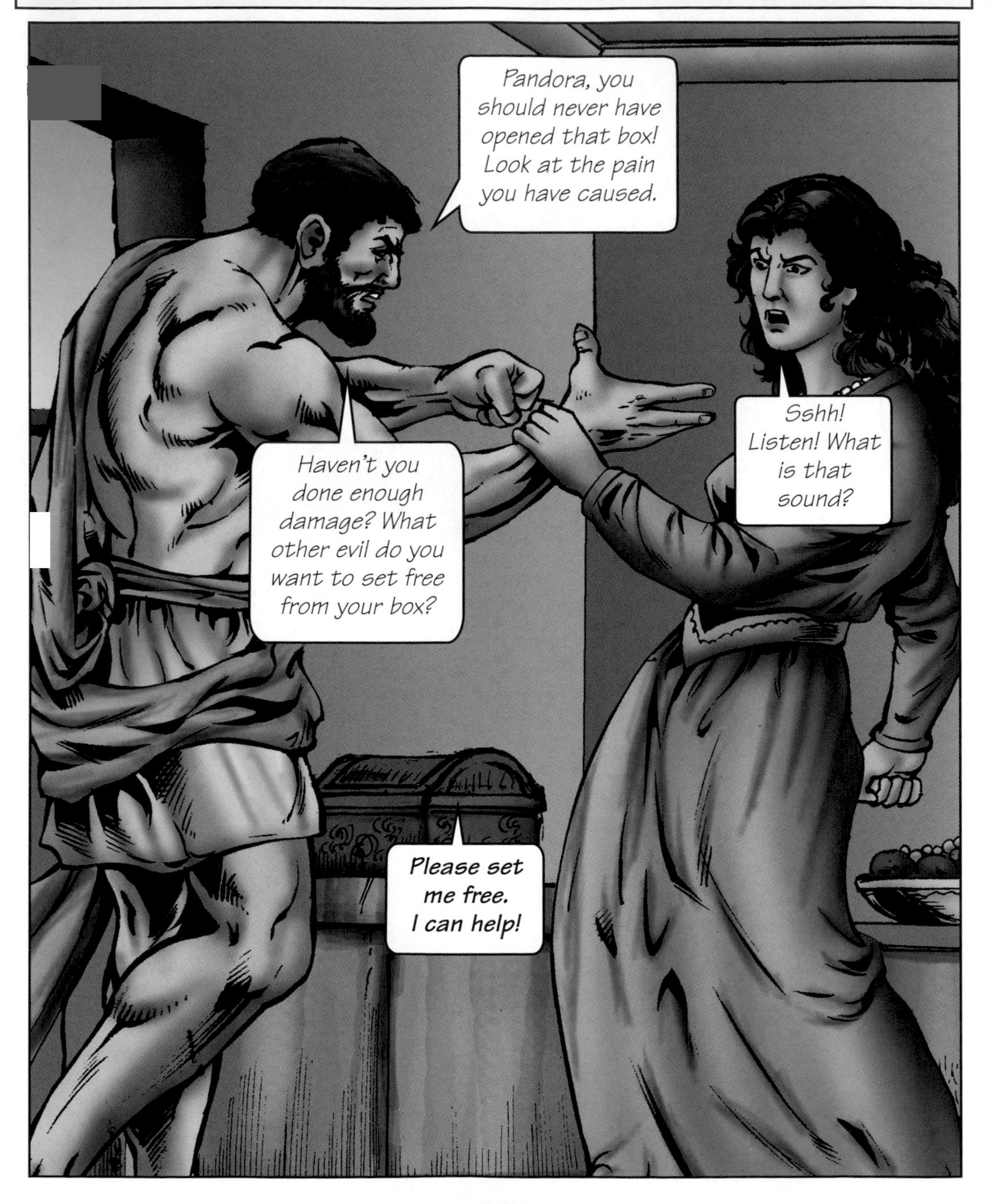

Soon, Epimetheus could also hear the voice. It was softer and sweeter than the other voices. Pandora and Epimetheus grew calm as the voice grew louder. Together, they decided that it was worth letting the creature out if it could help. They carefully opened the box. A tiny winged creature flew out. It was very different from the others.

Hera, what is this? Who dared to put Hope in Pandora's box?
Hope is all there is to fight the evils now on Earth.
Oh, Epimetheus. Look!
This creature is different. Maybe things will be all right again.
Free at last!
I am Hope! I will help you all feel better.

Hope fluttered around Pandora and Epimetheus, touching them and making them feel better. They began to smile and be friends again.

This is wrong. I don't want humans to feel anything good.
I feel so much better now that Hope is here.
Me, too! Everything seems brighter and happier now.

After bringing happiness to Pandora and Epimetheus, Hope flew out the window to help the rest of the world.

Goodbye, Hope! Try to make others feel better, too.
I know there is a lot of work for me to do.

Hope traveled far and wide, reaching all parts of the world. She brought relief from illness and pain wherever she went.

Hope brought happiness to everyone. Whatever evils they suffered, men could still look forward to a better future.

I feel stronger and better again.
I feel well again!

Pandora and Epimetheus now lived with hope. Whenever things went wrong, hope would help them. Soon they had a baby daughter called Pyrrha, who brought them great happiness.

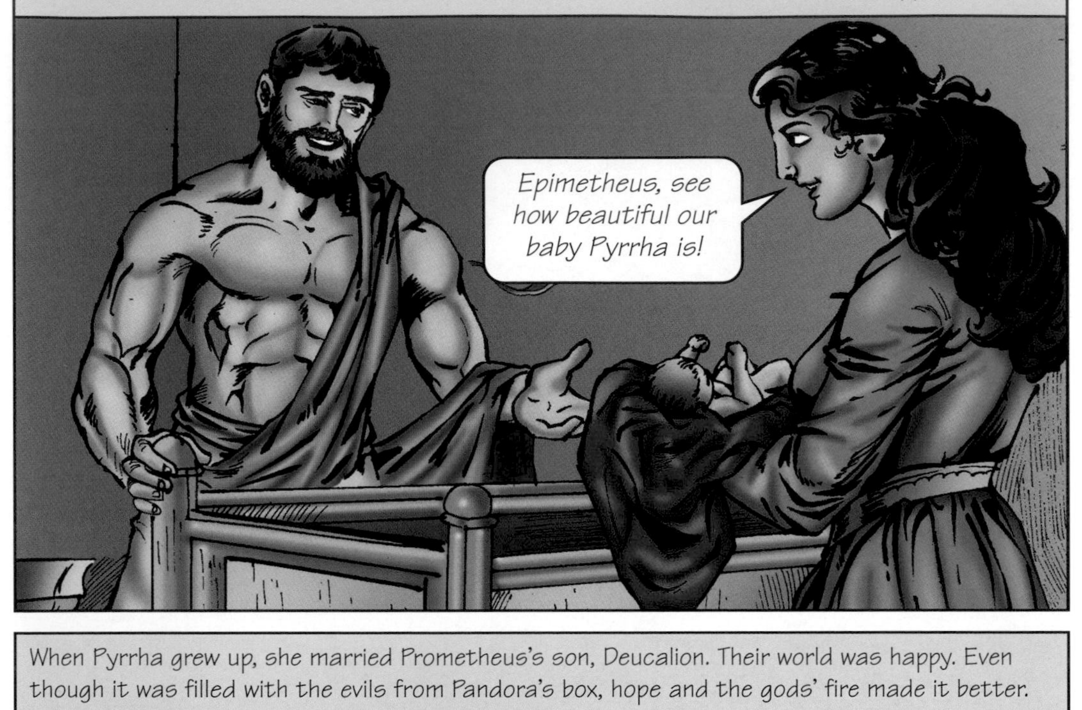

When Pyrrha grew up, she married Prometheus's son, Deucalion. Their world was happy. Even though it was filled with the evils from Pandora's box, hope and the gods' fire made it better.

Zeus was still angry. Hera begged him to stop punishing Prometheus for stealing the fire. But Zeus ignored her and sent fierce storms to flood the world.

The only people to survive the floods were Pyrrha and Deucalion. With Hope at their side, they set about rebuilding the human race.

FULFILLING ZEUS'S WISHES

The actions of Prometheus changed the world. It was now full of evils and death. But hope was always at their side. Was Zeus happy about what he had done?

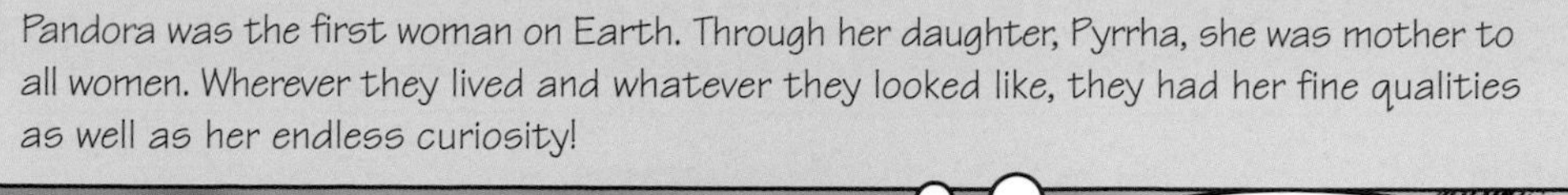

Pandora was the first woman on Earth. Through her daughter, Pyrrha, she was mother to all women. Wherever they lived and whatever they looked like, they had her fine qualities as well as her endless curiosity!

Pandora's final gift of Hope remained in the hearts and minds of all men and women forever. Hope was always there to lift their spirits and help them through bad times.

GLOSSARY

Aphrodite *daughter of Zeus and Dione and one of the twelve gods from Mount Olympus*

Apollo *son of Zeus and the Titaness Leto and one of the twelve gods from Mount Olympus*

Athena *daughter of Zeus who burst fully grown and armed for battle from her father's forehead; one of the twelve gods from Mount Olympus*

clay and water *the two basic components used by Hephaestus to make Pandora. They represent the Earth.*

curiosity *a desire to know or understand. For the ancient Greeks, curiosity could lead to good or evil.*

Deucalion *son of Prometheus and husband of Pandora's daughter Pyrrha*

dreams *according to the Greeks, a way the gods spoke to humans*

feasts *large gatherings of people eating together. It was an important feature of ancient Greek society. The Greeks believed the gods also held feasts.*

fire *a gift to humans that Prometheus stole from Olympus. Fire represented civilized life.*

floods *a weapon of Zeus, who was a weather god as well as king of Olympus*

funeral pyres *specially built bonfires on which the dead were laid and then burned as part of traditional Greek funeral rites*

Hephaestus *son of Zeus and Hera and one of the twelve gods from Mount Olympus*

Hercules *son of Zeus and the mortal woman Alcmena and the most famous hero of Greek mythology*

Hope *the last winged-creature or spirit that Pandora released from her magic box*

lyre *a stringed musical instrument common in ancient Greece*

mortal *able to die*

Mount Olympus *the home of Zeus's family of gods.*

pearls *natural gems that form inside the shells of oysters.*

Poseidon *son of Cronos and Rhea, Zeus's brother, and one of the twelve gods from Mount Olympus*

Pyrrah *daughter of Pandora and Epimetheus. She married Prometheus's son Deucalion.*

revenge *to get even for something done wrong to a person*

Titans *a race that ruled before Zeus and his family. They were giant creatures, the offspring of Uranus (Sky) and Gaia (Earth).*

voices *in Greek mythology, a way for the gods to influence humans*

vulture *a large meat-eating bird*

FOR MORE INFORMATION

BOOKS

Blood, Danielle. *15 Greek Myth Mini-Books.* New York: Instructor Books 2001.

Burleigh, Robert. *Pandora.* San Diego: Silver Whistle, 2002.

McMullan, Kate. *Keep a Lid on It, Pandora!* Myth-O-Mania: Book #6 (series). New York: Volo, 2003.

Weil, Lisl. *Pandora's Box.* New York: Atheneum, 1986.

WEB SITES

Pandora for Kids History for Kids - Europe, Asia, and Africa before 1500 AD
www.historyforkids.org/learn/greeks/religion/myths/pandora.htm
A simple retelling of the myth of Pandora

Encyclopedia Mythica: Pandora
www.pantheon.org/articles/p/pandora.html
The brief story of Pandora and links to information about other Greek characters

Publisher's note to educators and parents: Our editors have carefully reviewed these Web sites to ensure that they are suitable for children. Many Web sites change frequently, however, and we cannot guarantee that a site's future contents will continue to meet our high standards of quality and educational value. Be advised that children should be closely supervised whenever they access the Internet.

INDEX